You're Loaded

by

Dave Duell

Editor: Jay Randolph
Favor Communications International
P.O. Box 337287
Greeley, CO 80633

Layout: Wallace Ronne
Global Evangelistic Media Services
2527 49th Ave CT
Greeley, CO 80634
www.gemsmedia.org

Editorial Assistants: Bonnie Duell and Les Raley

Cover Design: Jeff Bristol

Published by Dave Duell Ministries

Table of Contents

The Spirit of Lack

As believers in Jesus Christ, there is no lack in us. We are complete in Him!

"And you are complete in Him, who is the head of all principality and power" (Col. 2:10).

If we are in Christ and He's in us, then who is the head of all principality and power? We are! Jesus has put all the principalities and powers under our feet. The only thing the devil can do now is just confuse us. The only way he can get to us is through what we don't know. But praise God, we're getting smarter and stronger daily through the revelation of God's Word. We aren't getting weaker. Our physical bodies may be aging, but on the inside we're getting stronger. We're becoming bold and taking our God-given place on the earth!

The Lord has given us authority to represent heaven. When we travel, we aren't just going to represent our country. It would be great to be an ambassador of the United States of America, but we have a higher rank than that. We're ambassadors for heaven! God's Word is in our mouth—and it's just as powerful in our mouth as it was in Christ's. We just have to go out there and be bold enough to speak it. The bolder you talk—the greater miracles you'll see!

Faithful Provider

We've been trained in lack our entire lives. That's because it all started with Adam and Eve. When they embraced the devil's lie, they opened a door to lack for all humankind.

Satan deceived them. He didn't just bluntly come out with His plans, but used the craftiest animal on the face of the earth instead. I find the fact that the devil used a talking snake pretty interesting. Have you ever wondered why this wasn't so unusual to Adam and Eve? Think about it. If a talking snake had come up to me, I would've been, "Whoa—a talking snake!" But maybe back then all the animals were talking. Whether they were or not, this spirit of lack has been on the earth since then.

We need to expose this age-old spirit of lack—and the only way we can do that is by knowing we are complete in Him!

A believer should never feel the sense of lack. On the surface, this sounds like an impossibility. Lack has been here so long that we just consider it normal. This world has trained us to be ruled by lack. However, lack shouldn't dominate us because we are complete in Him. Everything we need is already on the inside of us in our born-again spirit. God has given us EVERYTHING that pertains to life and godliness!

When you have abundance you feel good, but lack brings low self-worth. As Christians, our happiness doesn't depend on what we have in our billfold. We're rich because our Father is God. He owns the cattle on a thousand hills. Every once in a while we do have to ask Him, "Please sell a cow or two. We need some money!" However, we know God is our Faithful Provider.

Be of Good Cheer!

This idea that if you get to know God, life will be easy is false. Jesus Himself told us, **"These things I have spoken to you, that in Me you may have peace. In the world you will have tribulation; but be of good cheer, I have overcome the world"** (John 16:33). He said, "In this fallen world, you will have trouble." You don't even need a devil—life will give you all the problems you need! Adversity just shows up while you're living life.

The mother of a man in our church was recently promoted to glory. What a joy it was to have a Christian celebration service. Some tears were shed as she was remembered, but we weren't mourning as the world does. Mama went to heaven! How are you going to cry over that? She enjoyed eighty-seven years and raised some great kids. Praise the Lord!

Every one of us will get out of here someday. So why rush? We'll only be there forever. Until then, let's make a dent down here by doing what we're supposed to do while we're still around. Age has nothing to do with it. I'm never going to retire. I just re-fire! There's too much to do to even think about retiring. We're in our harvest. This is our time—our greatest hour! Jesus never promised us that everything would be perfect here on this earth. He recognized that we would encounter trouble, but His instructions were to be of good cheer. So encourage yourself—don't get down!

As we encounter these difficulties in life, it helps us to remember the big picture. First, God is our Father and He has an eternal plan for us. Is that awesome or what? God is voting for us, the devil is voting against us, and how we vote carries the election. I don't know about you, but I'm voting with God! We are more than conquerors with Him. We're His children and He loves us.

Second, this time on earth is just a training period. We're supposed to be training for our future with God by learning to trust Him down here. Tests come often to see whether or not we'll yield to Him and obey. Every problem we face is an opportunity to walk in faith and please God. Every challenge is a chance to overcome with His help.

Look Up

How can we expect to receive the rewards promised to an over-comer if we have nothing to overcome? Every time something comes up, we're overcomers—and there are blessings for overcomers. Something happens to a person who comes through the fiery furnace of a trial and doesn't even smell like smoke. When the Lord brings you through something impossible, you look back and say, "God delivered me once, and He can do it again!"

Many of the problems we get into are our own stupid mistakes, but God is Faithful. He doesn't say, "You stupid kid! Just go ahead and live through it yourself." The Lord isn't like that. He's with us!

We need to do what my little granddaughter does. She just comes along, grabs my pant leg, and looks up into my eyes. She never has to say anything like, "Pick me up, Grandpa." I just lift her up and she presses herself into me. That's what we need to do with God! When you grab His pant leg and look up into His face, He won't push you away. He'll pick you up, hug you, and hold you. Then you'll get His heartbeat running through you. You can't beat that!

When we're overwhelmed with trouble, all we need to do is look to Jesus. He's already won the victory. He has overcome the world, defeated the devil, and in Him is victory. According to Colossians 2:10, if victory is in Him, then it's also in us! **"Yet in all these things we are more than conquerors through Him who loved us"** (Rom. 8:37).

It's mostly a matter of focus. What are you thinking about? What God says in His Word will set you free and give you peace. God's Word is final, not all these temporary things that run through your brain. What the Lord says is eternal. Cling to His promises. Speak them, sing them, and shout them. Rejoice over God's Word and thank Him for keeping all of His promises.

In the midst of this, develop a closer relationship with Him. This is God's desire, and it should be yours too. Since relationships are based on communication, you must learn how to talk to God.

The House of God

So many Christians think that they have to "get holy" before they can approach God. They don't realize that when they were born again, they were given His righteousness and holiness as a gift. We call the Bible "holy" because His presence is in it. As saints, His Word and presence live inside us. This makes us holy too. God lives in a holy place—our born-again spirit. It's vacuum packed—sealed by the Holy Ghost. You can't get any more holy! (See my teaching entitled "*Awake to Righteousness.*")

We have believers trying to "get holy." Then they become "holey"—full of holes. If you look to your own "holiness," you'll just be full of holes and you'll never be able to keep the Holy Ghost in you. You'll leak!

But God has called us and put Himself in us. We are His temple today. The house of God isn't a building anymore. We are the house of God! Wherever you go, you're the house of God. You carry His Word and His presence. You can sing to yourself, preach to yourself, and even take up your own offering if you want. Give yourself a gift and then go buy yourself a steak!

Get in the habit of talking to God. He knows what you're thinking anyway! Just say, "Hey, Father!" You don't even have to call Him "Master" anymore. He's our Father. Speak freely and talk to Him like you do with your best friend. "You know what I'm going through. Please give me some help. I need Your help!" You don't have to be religious with God. He's not religious at all. The Lord just wants relationship with you.

Say, "No matter what I face, God is with me. I can overcome because Jesus has already won the victory. Hallelujah!"

"Strengthened"

"For this reason we also, since the day we heard it, do not cease to pray for you, and to ask that you may be filled with the knowledge of His will in all wisdom and spiritual understanding" (Col. 1:9).

What an awesome prayer to pray for each other! But it doesn't stop there.

"That you may walk worthy of the Lord, fully pleasing *Him*, being fruitful in every good work and increasing in the knowledge of God; strengthened with all might" (Col. 1:10-11).

"Strengthened" means "to make strong, confirm, enable." There is a family of *duna* power words. *Duna-mite* means "to be able." *Duna-mis* means "powers, usually supernatural." *Duna-moo* means "to strengthen." *Duna-tis* means "a sovereign, or ruler." *Duna-mato* means "to be mighty" and *duna-tos* means "powerful." All of that is in this word **"strengthened."**

We are **"strengthened with all might."** The Holy Spirit put this word in there to show us how we are strengthened. He used all the dynamite words—the power words. We are **"strengthened with all might, according to His glorious power, for all patience"** (Col. 1:11).

What was that? **"For all patience and longsuffering with joy"** (Col. 1:11). The joy of the Lord is our strength! **"Giving thanks to the Father who has qualified us to be partakers of the inheritance of the saints in the light. He has delivered us from the power of darkness and conveyed *us* into the kingdom of the Son of His love"** (Col. 1:12-13).

What Are You Going to Do?

We aren't just working to get into the kingdom—we're in it! I like how the *Message Version* states this:

"Be assured that from the first day we heard of you, we haven't stopped praying for you, asking God to give you wise minds and spirits attuned to his will, and so acquire a thorough understanding of the ways in which God works. We pray that you'll live well for the Master, making him proud of you as you work hard in his orchard" (Col. 1:9-10).

That's what we're doing—we're working in His orchard!

"As you learn more and more how God works, you will learn how to do *your* work. We pray that you'll have the strength to stick it out over the long haul—not the grim strength of gritting your teeth but the glory-strength God gives. It is strength that endures the unendurable and spills over into joy, thanking the Father who makes us strong enough to take part in everything bright and beautiful that he has for us" (Col. 1:10-12 *The Message*).

Isn't that good? Just when you think you can't make it, God's strength brings you through. (I address this in greater detail in my teaching entitled *"Throw Yourself A Party!"*)

You need to recognize that whenever you determine to live by faith, you'll be challenged. If you pursue something worthwhile, there will be opposition. You'll have to overcome obstacles. It's not just some dream world that we're living in. Although we might be headed for heaven, we're still dealing with life here on planet earth until then. Life on this fallen planet can give you all the difficulties you need even without the devil's input. Yet he throws his little tricks into the mix at times. There are plenty of things that seem to go wrong in life with or without him, but in the midst of these uncomfortable situations, you have to decide what it is you are going to do!

Complete in Him!

Praise God that He has provided everything we need to live happily and successfully in life! Even though this place is contaminated, we are the light of the world. We are the salt of the earth. God has sent us here to shine, preserve, and make it taste better. Faith is more of a way of walking than it is a way of talking. You have to walk out faith. There may be times when everything seems to go wrong in your life. Maybe the devil is whispering His lies in your ears and telling you you're defeated. He's saying, "There's no way out. You can't make it!" Please don't quit on his account. Your situation isn't truly hopeless. Remember, satan never tells the truth!

Whatever you're hearing in your head is a lie. The devil never tells the truth! So what are you going to do when these challenging situations come your way? Roll over and play dead? No! You're going to come alive!

I've been thinking about writing a book entitled "***Look Alive—The Buzzards Are Coming!***" The buzzards have easy pickins' with Christians. Come alive! For you to fail, God would have to fail. Yes, the enemy challenges your faith but that is to be expected. When you follow Jesus, you're always walking by faith. There's no way around it. Think back before you were born again. You walked with satan hand in hand, but now you're walking with God!

"Confirmation & Encouragement"

Personally, I just had another challenging week. I've had this stuff ringing in my ears: "Not going to make it! Defeated! You're going down!" But God has a way to encourage us.

Up until Wednesday night, it was all bad news. While sitting in my office praying, a man from back East called and asked, "How's it going, Dave?"

"Great, brother." (That was a faith statement)

The Lord used that man to encourage me. I thought about what he said for the rest of the evening. Then Thursday morning, Bonnie and I got up early at five. There was an email waiting for us from a friend in England. It had arrived at 4:52 am—just eight minutes before we checked it. That's God!

He wrote: "Hope this email finds you both well. In prayer this morning, I felt impressed to pray for you. (They're seven hours ahead) Normally I would keep this to myself, but I think this might be confirmation and encouragement. So this is what I got..."

"It's Done!"

(You can take this prophecy for yourself too. God is no respecter of persons)

"The Lord broke that burden on you through supernatural debt cancellation. The debt is gone. The heaviness is gone. Special angels are assigned to you to cause a money flow—not a trickle—but a flow to come from all directions."

"This is what God said, 'You are debt free.' Great is your joy, and happiness shall increase. Control is broken and leverage is given to you—especially through new open doors. They're new to you, but not new to the Lord. He set them in place before you were here. Mighty grace and virtue is released out of you as you praise God and believe it is so. It is so!"

"How does it all come to us? By believing it's so. You heard what God said. Now we have to believe it's so. Even though the circumstances may still keep coming, what did God say?"

"It's done. It's done! What you were praying for—it's done! It happened. It was done. It is so, and that's the end of that! No more shall it come near your doorstep ever again. Its back is broken. Now you have the victory—so rejoice, rejoice, rejoice and sense His awesome power at work."

"I thought I might send this to you." Praise God that he did!

"Rejoice!"

Then another friend sent us one later that afternoon. Hers was a confirmation too!

"I've been thinking about you guys a lot lately over the past few weeks. It's your turn! I saw a picture of a door being blown open. It was the Spirit of God blowing this door open for you. No man or devil can keep this from happening. I saw in the Spirit that both your vision and your team being very strategic for this end-time harvest. God has a plan. The devil tried to kill you and take everything away. He's attacked your flock and your family, but God says, 'It's your turn to see the salvation of the Lord!'"

"I believe these things are unfolding even now as I write this email. You have things to do by the Spirit of God. This is bigger than you think. Why do you think there has been such a fight? BUT GOD!!! His Spirit is going to blow this door wide open. The earth will be affected by the calling of God upon your lives. I just want to encourage you, Dave and Bonnie. I see it clearly. I feel the Spirit of God saying, 'Now is the time. Don't give up. Run to the finish line and take your prize!' I feel like the Lord is saying to you, 'I'm proud of you both.' I can see His face shining down on you. I love you, and I'm proud of you too!'"

Boy, that was just what we needed! You don't need some email saying, "You've had it!" God knows just how to encourage us! He never gets after you. He always lifts you up and encourages you that there is a way. Nobody is immune to these things. We all have challenges. Stuff happens, but God says, "Rejoice!"

Let's rejoice. That's what God wants us to do. Would you like to see some changes in your life? Start rejoicing! You'll drive the devil nuts! He's trying to drive you nuts. If you go the self-pity route, you will go nuts. You'll end up in a straitjacket—or killing yourself.

The moment you believe that there is one thing that God has not given you through the death, burial, and resurrection of Jesus, you have just committed to lack. Satan doesn't need you to deny Christ in order to destroy you. All he needs you to do is believe that what Jesus has given you isn't enough. We are complete in Him!

Immovable

Say that daily—"I am complete in Him!" Whenever circumstances show up in front of you, "I am complete in Him!" When you have that sense of wholeness, completeness, and righteousness that is based on the finished work of Jesus, you are immovable. Hallelujah!

That's the way God wants us to live. That's the way Jesus lived on the earth. He never had a sense of lack. All He had to do was look up into heaven. There it all was. Right there. He looked past all of the earthly circumstances. When He blessed the bread and fish, He looked up into heaven. There He was, looking at His Father sitting on the throne. God was saying, "It's all Yours. Whatever You need. It's Yours." That's when the miracle started happening!

We must look past our circumstances because we are already complete in Him. Once we buy into this lie of lack, we become open to every kind of temptation and emotional manipulation. Then this promise of joy and peace can't become a reality to us. We become trapped in the cycle of lack. The person who believes they are a new creation in Jesus never pursues the destructive process of "becoming." Instead, we reinforce the truth that we are and we can in Christ.

Think about it! When we start asking God for this and that, what does this prove? We're not believing! If you get a hold of this, it'll shorten up your prayers. Instead of asking the Lord for everything that we really do need, we can thank Him and say, "I am complete in Christ!" There's a revelation here that you need to receive. You are complete in Him!

When challenges, obstacles, and trouble show up in my life, "I am complete in Him." I choose to let the eternal truth of God's Word dominate my thoughts instead of the temporal facts of this natural realm. I don't pursue the destructive process of "becoming" because I already know that I am a brand-new creation in Him. As a believer, I reinforce the truth that I am, I have, and I can in Jesus.

Refocus

Lack makes you the center of every equation. Faith makes Jesus the center. We make rules to get out of sin, but instead, it brings us even deeper into it. The very thing we did to bring us life brings us death instead. The Bible reveals that **"the strength of sin *is* the law"** (1 Cor. 15:56) and **"whatever *is* not from faith is sin"** (Rom. 14:23). Instead of relying on the self-strength of your flesh, depend on God's glory-strength in your born-again spirit.

A simple decision to exalt God's Word above your experience will set you on the road to recovery from lack and launch you into a life of wholeness. This is the abundant life Jesus promised us. It's not avoiding the challenging circumstances of life—it's how we walk through them. That's the test. How will you come out the other side? **"Yet in all these things we are more than conquerors through Him who loved us"** (Rom. 8:37). Our sufficiency is in Christ. Everything we need is already inside us. We just need to refocus!

My six-year-old grandson told his mother, "I haven't learned a thing all summer. It's time to go to work. It's time to stop focusing on fun and start focusing on school!" Now that's the first time I've ever heard anything like that out of the mouth of a little boy. But it's true. We need to refocus. It's okay to have some fun in life, but let's focus on what God has to say!

One thing about the Lord is that He never drives us. He leads us. Psalm 23:1 says, **"The LORD *is* my shepherd; I shall not want."** Another translation renders this **"I shall not lack."** I like the *Message Version*. **"GOD, my shepherd! I don't need a thing."** What's this? Free from lack!

Paul wrote the Galatians, **"And because you are sons, God has**

sent forth the Spirit of His Son into your hearts, crying out, 'Abba, Father!'" (Gal. 4:6)

God didn't create us to be slaves. He has angels. He didn't want an army. He desired fellowship and family.

Love—Not Control

We usually think that the first relationship the devil messed up was God and man. However, you need to go back further than that. He messed up his own relationship with the Lord first, and then a third of the angels. If I ever get the chance, I want to ask one of those demons "Why did you fall for that?" They saw God. They were with Him. Yet, they followed in the rebellion of a created being.

Once Lucifer and the angels fell and came to earth, the first thing he wanted to do was mess up the relationship between Adam and Eve and God. He desired to disrupt the intimacy and harmony between the Father and His children, and he's still in the business of messing up relationships today!

I am a man of love. I love people, and love can overlook faults. However, what really bothers me is when Christians judge each other. God didn't call us to be charismatic sheriffs! **"Judge not, that you be not judged. For with what judgment you judge, you will be judged; and with the measure you use, it will be measured back to you"** (Matt. 7:1-2). I pour my life into people. I can't understand how one thing happens, and then Christians turn cold and treat each other like a piece of meat. They just throw their relationship over in the corner. That whole concept is just beyond me!

We're family—and we're going to live with each other forever! I realize that there are changes in relationships over time. I give people that. But there is a way to change. There is a proper way to cause a change in relationship. Changes happen in our lives all the time.

God didn't call spiritual leaders to dominate people. Yet, it's easy for them to fall into that trap. We came to set you free, and people who are free will eventually leave and go do other things for the kingdom. Our attitude is, "God bless you! See you in heaven!" The Lord has called us to love—not control—each other.

"I Made It!"

Life's not fair, but God is good. The Lord loves us!

When the Jewish leaders brought this woman who was caught in the act of adultery, Jesus just stooped down and wrote in the sand. Whatever it was He wrote, it sure caused quite a departure once He said, "Let him who is without sin throw the first stone!" Who was the only person in that situation without sin? Jesus. He was the only one who could have thrown the stone. Did He? No. God's love, grace, and mercy kicked into gear.

God has given that same grace to us. Therefore, we must extend grace to one another. Our job as believers is to build people up, not tear them down. Which sin is the worst anyway? In the Word, gossip is stuck right in there with murder. God doesn't grade on a curve. There is no curve—all are sinners. Isn't God's plan wonderful? He sees you and me perfect. Isn't that awesome? He sees us in Jesus and Jesus in us.

Even though all the works we did on our own apart from Him will be burned up on that day, the main thing is we get in! There'll be more excitement down at the gate than anywhere else. What fun it'll be to see the people come through who didn't think they would make it. They won't give a rip who's standing around watching how long and how loud they yell, "I made it! I made it! Hallelujah, I made it!"

Joy in God's Deliverance

"You are complete in Him, who is the head of all principality and power" (Col. 2:10).

The devil has no control. Jesus defeated him completely. He reduced him to a zero and knocked the rim off! God has blessed us so mightily, and we're finding out more and more how complete we really are in Him, what He's really done for us, what He's purchased for us, and what He's freely given to us. We are blessed above all peoples!

In knowing that we are complete in Him, there shouldn't be any lack in us—spirit, soul, or body. However, it seems like most people live off of lack.

Lack makes you the center of every equation. All you think about when you're in lack is "me." You don't think about blessing or looking out for somebody else. All you're looking out for is "me." But once you get rid of that old spirit of lack, you'll think of others.

Develop & Release

I want to give checks with more zeroes. I'm not one of these guys who say, "If I get more, then I can give less." No, no, no! Our job here is to make all the money we can to see how much we can give away. The only things you're going to keep forever are what you give away!

There is no lack in us, but lack stares us in the face like a giant. However, we're giant killers, and we can do it with the Word of God. We're finding out more and more how God has made us. One man said, "What you have undeveloped in you has no value." We are loaded with gifts and blessings. We just need to continue developing and releasing ourselves in Christ. Let the Holy Spirit expand you.

You must get by your brain. Your brain is like a stop sign. The enemy tries to stop you whenever the Holy Spirit comes on you and you need to move in Him. You need to learn to be obedient to the Holy Spirit because you have creative power in your voice.

While ministering just this week, I called out a word of knowledge: "Somebody here has bad shoulders, a hiatal hernia, and a blown out right knee." Other people came up for each one, but this one guy had everything. In one move of the Holy Spirit—in less than two seconds—he was instantly healed of all three. He jumped up on the platform and demonstrated his healed knee, which used to hyperextend. He said, "I hadn't golfed for four years because my shoulders were out of whack." It took a little guts to say, "Somebody has..." but you have to learn to speak.

Years ago, when I was still developing myself in this, I probably would have chickened out because I was always trying to preserve self. When you're ministering for Jesus, lay self aside and say what the Holy Spirit says. It doesn't make any difference what it is because God has someone's miracle in motion. If we'll say it, it'll happen. Glory to God!

Zero Hour

Have you ever had a zero hour? Zero hours are those bleak times in life, those lean seasons, those occasions when things seem to come to a dead end. Suddenly, there's no light at the end of the tunnel. If there is a light, it's probably another train coming. Everything seems to be upside down. You get to that point when you're tempted to say, "I'm ruined—done—finished. There's no hope." That's a zero hour.

Paul Milligan is a businessman from Texas who serves on Andrew Wommack's board. He has a company worth about a hundred million dollars. However, there was a time when he only had about four or five employees. He had a zero hour and everything got shut off. Paul walked into the kitchen and told his wife, "That's it, I've had it. We're done. I'm ruined. We're finished."

She didn't say much. She didn't respond, "Oh my God!" No. She just turned around and asked him, "Who told you to do this?"

"God did."

"Well, do you think that God is going to leave you here and ruin you? What's the big deal?" Paul worked through that time and came out of it.

"Whose Report Will You Believe?"

Then September 11th hit. Paul's company was worth about a hundred million dollars at the time. Everything stopped at September 11th. He works with big aircraft companies, and had something like 800 to 1,000 employees. Everything came to a halt because he had to have insurance. However, he couldn't get it. The only way he could keep his contracts was to get insurance, and nobody would cover him. His associate kept saying, "We need to get insurance. We don't have insurance. What are we going to do? We're going to have to call these companies and tell them we don't have insurance!"

Paul answered, "No, we're not! I've been there once before, and I'm not going there again." On the very last day before they had to call the companies, the clock ticked down to four in the afternoon. Then he heard an announcement over the speaker that so and so was wanted on the telephone, and he knew in his spirit that it was the insurance company. Paul heard his financial officer yell from his office, "YES!!!" and they threw a party. They had also thrown a party before this saying, "God isn't going to let us down." But it came down to a zero hour.

I had one about a year ago. I received a telephone call that left me under the impression that I was done, ruined, and finished in business. I sat there totally washed out—all hope was gone. What looked like a great victory totally deflated after that one phone call. Do you know what my wife asked me? Bonnie said, "Whose report will you believe? Are you going to believe the report of the Lord, or are you going to believe the report you just heard on the telephone?" Praise God for a woman of faith! My hope came back, and it wasn't but a day or two before everything changed. That was a zero hour. Have you had one?

If you are breathing, you could run into a zero hour. If you haven't had it yet, one is probably coming. I'm not prophesying bad over you. That's just life here on this fallen planet. Life isn't fair, but God is good. You don't even need a devil. Life will give you all the problems you need. But if you find yourself in that position, I have good news for you. Hold on! Christianity doesn't remove the red lights, stumps, setbacks, and tragedies, but it equips us for them.

Two Tornadoes

It's time for every born-again believer to realize that the purpose of Christianity isn't to teach us how to avoid every kind of difficulty, but to nurture within us the strength and character necessary for when these things come. God is building Himself in us. Something happens to a person when they come through the fiery furnace of a zero hour without even smelling like smoke. You come out the other side rejoicing.

Christianity doesn't make life easy. Rather, it provides the strength we need to face and overcome the trials of life. All men fail—but only the good ones get up and keep going!

Bob Nichols pastors a large church in Forth Worth, Texas. He experienced a zero hour with his congregation when two tornadoes collided right over their $13 million facility and smashed it to smithereens. There were about sixty people in the building at the time, and all of them were safe. When the two ladies in the prayer room opened up their eyes, the tornado had taken off the entire wall and they were looking out at the city. In spite of this tragedy, the next day the whole congregation was out there praising God publicly on television. It was a zero hour.

Almost three months before that, the Holy Spirit had prompted Bob saying, "Make sure you have all the insurance you need." So he went to his administrator and said, "Make sure we have all the insurance we can get on this place." That was God!

They argued and fought back and forth with the insurance companies. Back then they had a grade school and high school in their building. Finally, they came to a settlement. The insurance company said, "Why don't you take the land your building was on, sell it, and then go build a school." Well, that was thirteen prime acres downtown! So they ended up buying a nice place out on a four-lane highway and building a brand-new school.

The Open Door

Pier One liked their former land. As Bob talked with the chairman, they were offering a couple million lower than he wanted. So he said, "If you will give me what I'm asking for this land, we'll pray for your business, and it will increase and multiply because what you give me will go into a building for training children."

The chairman of the board responded, "You're the hardest man I've ever dealt with. But Reverend, we'll do it." So Pier One put up a $100 million building on that piece of property. The Lord turned that whole zero hour around. What looked like total disaster, God made awesome. Isn't He good!

The Lord honored Bob and Joy. They recently celebrated forty years of pastoring that church and fifty years of marriage. President Bush sent them his congratulations. The mayor gave them the key to the city. They were flown in on Ross Perot's helicopter. The Nichols were honored like nobody else! God turned that zero hour into a blessing they couldn't have even imagined!

This is what you have to see. When one door closes in life, so many people stand there staring at that door instead of looking around for the one that's opened. Get your eyes off of the door that closed and turn them to the one that's open. Guaranteed, there will be an open door!

You have immeasurable power living on the inside of you. All power has to have a power source. We have the Holy Spirit—the One who created everything, including us—inside, and we go walking around acting like we don't have anything. That's blasphemy against the Holy Spirit! The way you ought to pray is by walking around saying, "I'm loaded, I'm blessed, I'm gifted, I'm complete in Him!" That blesses Jesus and the Holy Spirit on the inside of you. Going around saying, "I don't have this, I don't have that," and begging God for stuff proves that you don't believe that you are complete in Him. Once you get a revelation of what I'm talking about, it'll shorten up your prayers.

"Patience Will Pay"

What you've been praying for, you already have. That's what the Bible says! Second Peter 1 says that He's given us everything that pertains to life and godliness ACCORDING TO the knowledge we have of Him. That's your answer right there. Ignorance is expensive! What you don't know is where the devil is getting you. That's why it's so important to study the Word.

You need to find out who you are and what you have in Christ. Then you'll start walking around like Jesus did—enjoying abundant life. It won't make any difference what zero hour comes your way. You'll both have and live the abundant life.

When Jesus woke up the morning of His crucifixion, I believe He was singing, "This is the day, this is the day, that the Lord has made, that the Lord has made. I will rejoice, I will rejoice, and be glad in it, and be glad in it." He was already seeing past the cross.

You need to see what your faith will produce. You need to focus on the end result. Don't let failure stop you. Just keep walking. Warfare always surrounds the birth of a miracle. Failure isn't an event anyway. It's just an opinion.

Colossians 1:9-11 says that we pray this **"that you may be filled with the knowledge of His will in all wisdom and spiritual understanding; that you may walk worthy of the Lord, fully pleasing *Him,* being fruitful in every good work and increasing in the knowledge of God;**

strengthened with all might, according to His glorious power, for all patience and longsuffering with joy."

God told me years ago, "Patience will pay." Everything we need has been given to us freely. If you need patience, you have all the patience you need on the inside of you. All the joy you need is on the inside of you. It's in there. It's just your brain that tries to get ahead, say, "It must not be God," or whatever. The Lord is working, so just keep walking. Keep taking those steps of faith and you'll find out where God lives. Just keep believing! There's always joy in God's deliverance. Always! The joy of the Lord is your strength.

Perspective

"Being confident of this very thing, that He who has begun a good work in you will complete *it* until the day of Jesus Christ" (Phil. 1:6).

Who's going to perform it? He is! We just have to keep moving forward by faith. Remember what the Lord told the children of Israel in the wilderness? "Keep moving! Pick yourself up and keep going!" There are zero hours, but I can do all things through Christ who strengthens me. I let this mind be in me also that was in Christ Jesus. What mind was that? The mind of Jesus Christ! His mind is in our born-again spirit. He gives us instructions and encouragement every day. We have a God who guides and encourages us. Aren't you glad He doesn't give up on us? Aren't you glad He doesn't yell out of heaven, "You stupid so and so!" God loves us!

If the Lord fell off His throne every time we made a mistake, He'd be laying on the ground all the time. Pick yourself up, dust yourself off, and throw yourself a party. We have a God who is loaded and blessed. He's not sick or broke. He's not up in heaven saying, "Oh Myself! How am I going to pay the note on the throne?" If God be for you, WHO can be against you? NO ONE! Meditate on this a little bit. If God be for us, who can be against us? That means we can't fail. It may look like we failed, but that's just somebody's opinion. Keep moving forward in faith!

The Stupidity of It All

Consider a football game. There are twenty-two guys on the field playing their hearts out. They're all playing hurt. If you got slammed around every day like they do, you'd have pain somewhere in your body too. But they just get up and go. Only Christians give up when they're hurt. They whine, "So and so offended me. I'm not going back to church!" How dumb can you get and still breathe? Your dipstick doesn't touch oil! Every believer needs to fellowship with other Christians.

So there are twenty-two men working hard out on the field in dire need of rest, and 72,000 people sitting in the stands in dire need of exercise. Up in the bleachers, they're all coaches. They're up there drinking their beers and downing their hot dogs, yelling, "That stupid guy! He fumbled the ball!" I wonder what you'd do if they hit you that hard. It's a miracle they hang on to that thing!

Here's the stupidity of it all. Football is basically twenty-two overpaid young men in a $50 million stadium fighting over a little $100 pigskin. There's not too much sense to that, but I love it!

Theodore Roosevelt said, "The credit belongs to the man who is actually in the arena, whose face is marred by dust and sweat and blood. Who strives valiantly, who errs and comes short again and again. Who knows the great enthusiasm, the great devotion, and spends himself in a worthy cause. Who at his best knows in the end the triumph, the high achievement, and who at his worst, if he fails, at least he fails while daring greatly."

That's the kind of person I want to be!

"Temporary!"

This life we're in is just temporary. The situations you find yourself in right now are temporary. God gives you a vision, and the next thing you know you find yourself in a pit saying, "Lord, where'd the vision go?" No matter what hits you or comes your way, you must get the vision on the inside of you.

Look at Joseph. God showed him a vision, and he blabbed it to his brothers. The next thing you know, he's in a pit. He looked up out of that pit and yelled, "Temporary!" Joseph knew he wasn't going to finish up in a pit. His vision would get him out of there.

Are you in a pit? Maybe you need to yell, "Temporary!" Come on! That's not going to get you out of the pit. Say it with some enthusiasm. "TEMPORARY!!!" When you're in a zero hour, your turbocharger kicks in.

Joseph got out of the pit, but the next thing he knew he was marching toward Egypt in chains as a slave. All along the way, he was saying, "Temporary, temporary, temporary." Got a nice job, but his master's wife tried to get him in bed. He ran, but she grabbed his coat. The next thing he knew, he was in prison for that. "Temporary!" You know the rest of the story.

Remember when Joseph was standing naked on the auction block? Potiphar, in his nice robes, stood nearby assessing him. Which one did God call prosperous? That's right—Joseph, the naked slave. He had prosperity working on the inside of him (Gen. 39:1-4). He carried his vision—the one God gave him—in his heart.

Enforce His Victory

We are complete in Him. We have prosperity—and everything else we need—on the inside of us. You don't even have to pray "up." I hear Christians say, "My prayers don't even get through the ceiling." Well, they don't have to. That's why we bow our heads. He's in our spirit man/belly. We don't have to pray to "open up the heavens." Jesus opened the heavens to believers over two thousand years ago!

Warfare is when two undefeated foes fight each other. Therefore, the fight of faith that believers wage shouldn't really be called "spiritual warfare." Why? Because satan is a defeated foe! Jesus won the victory two thousand years ago and gave us the spoils. We're not heading toward a victory, we're coming from one. We're already victors in Christ. God is just looking for someone bold enough to believe Him who will open up their mouth and start using the authority we've been given to enforce that victory on earth.

31

"And we know that all things work together for good to those who love God, to those who are the called according to *His* purpose" (Rom. 8:28).

Do you love God? Are you called according to His purpose? Yes? Then you can be sure that God is working all things together for good in your life.

Use Your Spiritual Eyes

Consider Paul. He went through something like seventy-two major difficulties, including being stoned. Now when somebody was stoned back then, they died. They didn't just use some little pebbles to deliver a few knocks on the head. They put the person being stoned down in a pit and then threw boulders down on their head until their brains oozed out. Paul died, but God raised him from the dead! (Acts 14:19-20)

Paul was beaten with rods and shipwrecked, but most of us haven't even been spit on yet—and we want to quit? We need to change our perspective!

"For our light affliction, which is but for a moment, is working for us a far more exceeding *and* eternal weight of glory, while we do not look at the things which are seen, but at the things which are not seen. For the things which are seen *are* temporary, but the things which are not seen *are* eternal" (2 Cor. 4:17-18).

We're spirit-beings. We walk by the spirit. We should see by the spirit. When these challenging circumstances come, we need to use our spiritual eyes to see past them. When Jesus prayed for the loaves and the fish to multiply, He looked up into heaven past all the temporal circumstances and saw Father God saying, "Yes!" That's what we need to see!

Throw Yourself A Party!

Consider these same verses in the *Message*:

"So we're not giving up. How could we! Even though on the

outside it often looks like things are falling apart on us, on the inside, where God is making new life, not a day goes by without his unfolding grace. These hard times are small potatoes compared to the coming good times, the lavish celebration prepared for us. There's far more here than meets the eye. The things we see now are here today, gone tomorrow. But the things we can't see now will last forever" (2 Cor. 4:17-18).

That'll put a shout in a statue—praise God! Paul put all these things into perspective. Jesus said, "When these things happen, jump up and shout for joy—for great is your reward in heaven!" James said:

"My brethren, count it all joy [Throw yourself a party!] when you fall into various trials, knowing that the testing of your faith produces patience" (James 1:2-3; brackets mine).

You need to become a party-person. It'll drive the devil nuts! He's trying to drive you nuts all the time through all kinds of people, places, and things. You can equip yourself now for when the next zero hour comes. You can already have made up your mind about what you're going to do. Throw yourself a party!

"Perfect, Complete, Lacking Nothing"

"But let patience have *its* perfect work, that you may be perfect and complete, lacking nothing" (James 1:4).

It's God's will that you be perfect and complete, lacking nothing. He wants all your needs to be abundantly met. That's what this means. So if we respond properly to any test, trial, or temptation, we'll come out on the other side perfect, complete, and lacking nothing.

God is no child abuser! He doesn't use the devil to "train" us. He is quite able to teach us Himself.

We live in a world where the enemy is out after our souls. He wants to attack us. We need to learn how to use our spiritual authority and weapons to defeat him. It's really important for you to learn how to stand your ground in a day of trouble. God likes you to stand tall and not fall.

33

Jesus has overcome the devil, and so can we. The Lord has made a way out for you!

"But Dave, I thought you said that somehow the bad things that happen to us are going to work out to make us better in the end? Should we just let the devil run over us, steal from us, and flatten us?" That's how religion has interpreted these promises.

Pray Without Ceasing

Many old-time Pentecostals would glorify heaven in this way. They thought that if they arrived in heaven beaten, bloody, and completely defeated, that this would somehow bring more glory to God and to them. No! The Lord wants us to run into heaven shouting and jumping for joy!

I remember hearing some pitiful old songs. "It will be worth it all in the sweet by and by. It will all be over if we just hold on 'til the end." Another one went, "So foot sore and poorly shod, but at the end of the journey, there's God." But the worst I ever heard was, "Sick, sober, sorry, and broke. Disgusted and sad, I gave my life to Jesus and lost everything I had." That sure doesn't sound like faith to me!

When we go through things, we need to recognize that God has already put everything we need on the inside of us to be able to overcome. All the gifts of the Holy Spirit are in you. All the fruit of the Holy Spirit—including joy and peace—are in you. You might not have seen them yet, but they're in you. They'll develop. You just need to have the right kind of teaching so you can have a full, balanced, and happy life.

You can pray without ceasing. "Oh Dave, I can't do that!" Yes, you can. If you can worry without ceasing, you can pray without ceasing. That's why God gave us tongues. You can pray in the Spirit all day and all night if you want. Even when you're talking to someone else, these supernatural words will roll like a river on the inside of you. Have you noticed that? It's your spirit praying to God—without ceasing, praying perfect, opening up doors for you, praying for yourself and others. You'd be shocked to know what you're praying for in tongues. What an awesome way to pray!

A Heart of Love

Confess God's Word in your situation. Jesus did. When the devil showed up, He said, "It is written…" That's what you and I need to say. "It is written…" God's covenant Word is powerful coming out of your mouth. The power of God is strongest in a believer's mouth. You need to learn how to talk!

Live your life for others. Walk in love and forgiveness. When you put others before yourself—loving, giving, and sowing good things into their life—you'll begin to see it all come back to you in good measure, pressed down, shaken together, and running over. Let love and kindness flow from your life.

You can go anywhere in the world with a heart of love. Anywhere! It's not what you know or how well you can speak. It's whether you love the people. All that matters is how you are leaving that person after they walk out of your life. Are you leaving them sad, happy, or what? We're supposed to be like Jesus. Let the love of God flow out of our lives. People need that. Always leave a person or situation better than when you first arrived. Learn to forgive instantly no matter what it costs you in the long run.

Walk in righteousness. You are righteous. When you know that you have peace with God, you can walk around like Jesus saying, "I have peace with God. I am the righteousness of God in Christ Jesus." You need to look in the mirror and say, "You righteous thing, you!" Keep saying it until you believe it because you are righteous in God's sight because of Jesus. Fall in love with Him.

The Holy Spirit is an honored guest on the inside of you. Imagine having an honored guest living in your house all the time. How would you treat them? That's the way you have the Holy Spirit on the inside of you. You need to think about that. When the enemy comes your way, say, "I have an honored guest on the inside of me, and I'm not going to dishonor my guest." Put the Gospel first in all you do. Give generously of your prayers, time, and finances. Get the big picture of what life is all about.

He's Worthy!

Instantly obey every prompting of the Holy Spirit. If you get an impression, hunch, or leading, go ahead and do it. I carry a $100 bill in my pocket. I'm waiting to buy someone's groceries in front of me sometime when their credit card doesn't work or they don't have any money. I'll say, "Don't worry about it. I'll buy your groceries." You can always be a blessing to somebody!

At lunch during our men's conference, we tipped our waiter $140. That was bigger than the bill! The guy said, "You're giving me $140!"

"Yes, sir. We just want to bless you today, young man. Jesus loves you, and we love you too." I bet he hasn't stopped talking about that yet. "These guys gave me a tip bigger than their bill!"

Be a worshiper of God. Worship Him with all you are and all you have. It's great when you feel God, but it's also great when you don't. You can't live life on feelings. You'd be a mess! Andrew Wommack had a three-month time with the Lord that almost ruined him. When the feeling left, he thought God had died and he wanted to die too. So he went around asking the Lord to kill him. We're not made to live in that kind of feeling all the time. We'll be in heaven someday, but right now we live by faith.

When God wanted to be close to His children in the Old Testament days, He said, "Gather your tents and bring them around Mine." He wants family more than anything. He desires relationship. So be a good kid. Be a good family member. His presence is in you right now. Acknowledge Him, thank Him, and praise Him. He's worthy!

Getting Started

There's nothing greater in all the world than seeing Jesus change people's lives! When the Holy Spirit touches someone, it can happen in a second. It's awesome to know that you and I get to represent heaven. Wherever we go, we re-present Jesus. We can affect everyone we bump into—even when we're sleeping!

I was flying to California a few years ago. Since it was early in the morning, I stretched out in my aisle seat, and fell asleep. When I woke up, the eyes on the African-American fellow sitting next to me were as wide as saucers. Apparently, he'd been waiting for me to wake up. Immediately, he asked, "Who are you?"

"What do you mean, brother?"

"I stepped over you to go to the bathroom and I froze. I couldn't move. Nothing would operate. I had to have a stewardess pull me over. Then the same thing happened when I returned and went back over you. What is that?"

"That's the Holy Ghost, brother!"

"Holy Ghost? What do you mean?"

And I told him. He was saved in a couple of minutes, and then became baptized in the Holy Spirit just like that! God is awesome!

Chief Servant

We travel with the Power Team—Father, Son, Holy Ghost, and a host of angels! You may feel all by yourself, but you're loaded. You're blessed. God has chosen us to work His power through. Isn't that amazing? Glory to God! I just can't get over how the Holy Spirit causes the Word of God to come alive to us. That's what He did for me with Colossians 2:10. **"And you are complete in Him, who is the head of all principality and power."**

We are complete in Him. As you continue meditating on this truth, the Holy Spirit will reveal His Word to you.

Everyone comes from different places. You may think, *Dave has it made!* Well, you don't know what it's taken for me to be where I am today. I was a farmer and a rancher. Bonnie and I thought that's what we were going to do for the rest of our lives, but God had a different plan.

I'm the youngest of thirteen children. I barely made it! But when I was born, my mother looked at me and said, "This is our preacher." Out of all the kids, I was the only one she said that to. My Dad passed that around in all the sale barns saying, "We have our preacher!" I didn't know that for many years, but praise God, the Lord had a call on my life. My mother prophesied that into me, but it took me awhile to discover it.

Do you want to find out the call God has on your life? Just be chief servant. Serve people. Do you want to get where God wants you to be? Just keep serving. That's the greatest thing you can do. God will reveal things to you as you bump up against and serve other people. The anointing is more caught than taught, so just keep serving.

That's what Bonnie and I did. In fact, that's still what we're doing today. Ministry is just serving people. We're here to be chief servants.

Changed My Life!

It's interesting to see how the Holy Spirit guides and directs your steps. You don't see it at the moment, but you could look back and see the thread of the Holy Spirit going through every situation in your life. I was baptized in the Holy Spirit when I was thirty. I went to a church that didn't talk about being baptized in the Holy Spirit. In fact, they didn't talk much about the Holy Spirit at all.

Our church was so dead that one Sunday morning a guy died in the service. They called 911, and the emergency crew came and took out half the church before they found the dead guy. You just have to get hungry!

I started reading the Book. Pastors don't have any problem preaching about Jesus' miracles. But they do have a problem when it comes back to the questions "Are you experiencing God's power?" and "Have you seen these things?" I wanted to see these things. I longed to see this Bible come alive.

So I asked the Holy Spirit, "What's the problem?" Guess what? When you seek, you'll find. When you knock, the door will be opened to you. I bought a horse from a guy—sight unseen—who was a charismatic. My people warned me about them. They said, "Those folks will make you crazy!" While hanging around these people, I found out that they were having more fun than I was. So I received the Baptism in the Holy Spirit. Changed my life! Changed my thinking! Changed everything!

You Go By Faith!

I began to pray for sick cows and horses. They're the easiest to pray for. They never argue with you. They just get it. Praise God! All you have to do is lock a cow into the chute. I could make a fortune selling little "sheep" chutes for pastors' offices. When people come in for counseling, the pastor could just have them go down on their hands and knees and lock their head in the chute. Then they could work on their head for a little bit. Maybe a sanctified kick would be in order. It would definitely shorten up pastoral counseling sessions! If I patented and marketed this, I could become an instant millionaire. I'd scare the hell out of a lot of people when they came into my office, pointed to the chute, and asked, "What's that?"

"It's where you're going next!"

So anyway, I was praying for sick cows and horses. I led a lot of ranchers and other people to the Lord this way. Things were happening. While at the National Western Stock Show in Denver one afternoon, I looked up and saw a great big ball of color. I told the other cowboys I was with, "Hey, look at that!" They couldn't see it. Only I could see it. Then, after eating dinner and attending a sale, we went up to our hotel room and praised God for four or five hours.

A prophecy came to my mouth. I said, "God, if that was You, verify it!" All five of us in the room immediately hit the deck. Then we got up and started talking about what we saw. The next thing we knew, we heard a mighty rushing sound—like a tornado. However, I told them, "It can't be a tornado! It's Denver in January!" This sound wasn't outside, it was inside. So we listened to the Holy Spirit in the wind for over an hour. He'd come and go. That's when God spoke to me and said, "I'm giving you a ministry called 'Faith Ministries.'" I didn't know faith from hope! But God did. Three or four years later, we started finding out what it was all about—hallelujah!

God said, "I want you to start a church."

I said, "What?"

We had a regular Bible study with a bunch of college students. I told my wife, "I think this thing is turning into a church."

She said, "That's the dumbest thing I've ever heard. Besides that, who would be the pastor?" Hey, I just want to let you know where I came from. My wife wasn't exactly shouting with joy. She wouldn't even come to my meetings. Many of the college students didn't even know I was married! She said I was flaky. I was going out and giving my testimony. You need to know this because you don't just go on goose bumps. You go by faith!

"Just Enough Word"

Have you ever noticed that right before you go to church or a meeting, World War III breaks out? Do you have that problem? Be honest. On one particular day, I was preparing to leave for one of my first meetings. I think the cat got in the house or something like that. But I didn't have brains enough to stay there and get it settled. I said, "I have a meeting to go to." As I was just about ready to get into the car, I heard my wife yell from the house, "HYPOCRITE!" Oh how the anointing just flows from that word—the wrong anointing. I drove down the road with that word ringing in my ears.

I went to the meeting, and put a smile on my face. "Hallelujah. Good to see you, brother!" My testimony that night sounded to me like the dullest thing I'd ever heard. Then I asked, "Anybody here need healing?" I had to say that because I had told God I would. The whole place stood up. People got healed everywhere. I thought, *How is this working?* On the ride home I asked, "How'd You do that?"

The Holy Spirit answered, "You gave just enough Word for people to believe Me. I'm backing up the Word—not your goose bumps!" That's Burning Bush University. That's how it works. That's how we got into all this.

Yellow Cadillac

We started a church in our hometown. Jesus warned about that. Your relatives are the ones who give you the most "encouragement." I won some businessmen to the Lord who were broke. They started prospering and then bought us a brand-new yellow Cadillac. That's hard on Christians. It was hard on my wife! She wouldn't accept it. I came home so excited because we were driving a Toyota that you could see the ground in. My wife could have lost her purse through the hole in that floorboard! Then these guys gave us a new Cadillac. She was excited, but also suspicious. Bonnie asked, "What kind of car did they give us?"

I answered, "A brand-new yellow Cadillac."

"Cadillac! I'm not going to ride in that thing! What are people going to say?"
I was thinking, *Who gives a rip?* She made me go to our Presbyterian pastor and ask him what he would do. I said, "Dr. McIntosh, I have a problem. Some people want to give us a brand-new Cadillac. My wife

has sent me here to ask you what you would do."

He stroked his little old goatee and said, "Well, you go home and tell your wife that if she doesn't want it, I'll take it!" I reached over and kissed that old man. Hallelujah! I felt like that Native American chief. He rode the horse while his squaw was following behind. Somebody asked him, "How come your wife is walking?"

He answered, "She doesn't have a horse." That's what I was thinking about Bonnie, *She didn't have a car!* I just want to let you know where we came from. You have to get started somewhere—praise God!

Holy Ghost Travel Agency

I remember when I was just filled with the Holy Spirit. I felt like the father of the girl whom Jesus raised from the dead in Don Francisco's song: "I Gotta Tell Somebody!" I was sitting there in my living room saying, "I gotta tell somebody!" And the Holy Spirit said, "Hey Dave, do you want Me to be your travel agent?" Pay attention: This may be a clue from the Lord for you. I asked, "You would be my travel agent?" He answered, "Yep. Holy Ghost Travel Agency. I'll set up every meeting for you for the rest of your life." I said, "Glory to God!" It works. I've been to seventy-three countries in the past thirty-plus years. Never asked for a meeting—glory to God! Thank You, Father.

God told me, "I'm going to have you travel so much that you'll have to look at the hotel phone to see where you're at." That's actually happened to me. I've woken up and said, "I don't know where I am." I had to go over and look at the telephone to find out. It's been a thrill to work for the Holy Spirit!

Are You Listening?

When God made Adam and Eve, He didn't put them out in the desert. He prepared a place for them where all five senses were satisfied. All their needs were met in the garden. They had zero sense of lack until that talking snake showed up.

If I was in the Garden of Eden and a snake came up and said, "Hey, how's it going?" I would have exclaimed, "A talking snake!" Then I would have run and gotten Adam, saying, "Look, a talking snake!" Think about it. On the other hand, maybe this wasn't such a big deal. Maybe there was a whole bunch of talking animals there.

So where did this sense of lack come from? The snake. He put that sense of lack into Adam and Eve. He made them believe that God was holding back something. He did it so deceptively that we can't blame Adam and Eve too much. We've all fallen for the same trick. That old sense of lack is still ruling most of us today.

There shouldn't be any sense of lack in any Christian. God has already given us everything that pertains to life and godliness (2 Pet. 1:3). If we truly believed that, it would shorten up our prayers. Do you know what I am now? Eternally grateful! God loves prayers like, "Thank You, Lord. You've given me everything I need!" Doubt and unbelief prays, "Oh

God, what am I going to do today? I don't have everything working in my life." Faith prays, "I'm loaded. I'm blessed. I'm complete in Christ—I don't need a thing!"

Our brain tries to figure everything out, but we need to learn how to walk by the Spirit. We are Spirit-creations. We should learn to walk by the Spirit greater than walking by our brain. Listen to the Holy Ghost!

"Hide & Go Seek"

Another man and I received the Baptism in the Holy Spirit at about the same time. We were working together. I said, "I don't know about you, but I'm not hearing the Holy Ghost."

He answered, "Me either."

So I told him, "This is what we'll do. We're going to play Hide & Go Seek in the Holy Ghost. You get in your pickup and go hide somewhere in town. I'll ask the Holy Spirit where you are. This is how we'll practice listening to Him." So he took off in his pickup, and I sat there in mine praying, "Where's Don? Oh God, where is Don? Holy Spirit, You'll have to speak louder than that. I can't hear a thing. I don't hear anything." My radio was turned off, but I heard nothing.

Finally, I just became frustrated, started the pickup, and took off. I drove up and down every street and alley trying to find him. Eventually, I ran into him by accident. So I told him, "Now it's your turn." We did that two or three times a week, and started hearing the Holy Spirit. After six months, town was too small. So we used the entire county! We'd make it hard on each other by going through gates and hiding in trees. That's how I learned to hear the Holy Spirit. I practiced with my friend!

We don't spend enough time practicing! Doctors practice medicine. They practice, practice, and practice some more. If you go to them, they'll practice on you. No matter how much wisdom and experience they have, they're still just practicing. I'm not against doctors, but if you die, they'll keep right on practicing. However, many Christians quit praying for the sick just because Sister So and So died.

This happened in the Presbyterian church we attended. The husband fasted and prayed forty days. I went up to see this lady three days before she died. People don't know the truth. I went in there and said, "I see Jesus coming. I don't know if He's coming to heal you or to take you home." She said, "Oh, I pray it's to take me home!" That was her prayer. She didn't want to stick around. Guess what? She went home. This nailed that Presbyterian church. People quit praying and just kind of gave up.

No Credit

You have to learn to keep going because it isn't you doing the healing anyway. I learned this the hard way myself. When I thought I was "God's man of faith and power," I told my wife, "I'm going to go empty the hospital." She said, "You go. I'll pray for you."

So I went up there saying, "I'm God's man of faith and power. I just saw a miracle!" Although I started on the top floor and worked my way down, not one person followed me out healed. So I sat down in the waiting room and asked, "God, what's the problem?" It's good to ask questions sometimes.

He answered, "Dave, who's doing the healing?"

"Well, not me. I've definitely proved that."

"Could you take any credit if they got healed?"

"No."

What He told me next changed my life forever: "Neither can you take any credit if they don't get healed."

That's where the devil comes in and puts condemnation on you. He says, "You don't have anything." No, you're loaded! Say, "I am complete in Him. Praise God, all the gifts of the Holy Spirit are inside of me. The very same power that raised Christ from the dead lives in me." We walk around in ignorance and unbelief, blaspheming the Holy Ghost and acting like we don't have anything. We're loaded!

45

God's Answer Man

You'll see greater things happen in your life if you start talking right. "I'm loaded. Anybody need any answers? I got 'em. I'm God's answer man." The Holy Spirit is inside of you and He knows everything. All you have to do is listen. Then let the Holy Ghost talk by opening your mouth and wiggling your lips. Your ears will wrap around your head and say, "Wow—that's good!"

I was sitting in an airplane flying to Tulsa. This other guy and I were the only two people in first class. We had a steward who was attending to us, whom I found out right away was a Baptist. I looked over at this young guy and said, "Do you mind if I come over and sit by you? We're just up here by ourselves. I'd like to talk to you."

He answered, "Sure, come on over."

I asked him, "Are you happy, brother?"

He answered, "It's strange you would ask me that. I just went up in the mountains with my wife and two little boys yesterday. I make money in the six figures, but I was telling my wife 'I am not happy, but I'm going to find out what'll make me happy.'"

I said, "Congratulations, young man. I'm your answer man. This is a set up by God. You asked God and now I have all your answers. Start asking questions."

"That Must Be Dave"

"What makes you happy?"

"Good question!" The Baptist came and listened to me tell this guy about Jesus. He watched the young man get born again. Then I said, "Brother, there's more. You need to be baptized in the Holy Spirit!"

"What's that?"

"It's the power! You speak in tongues and..." About that time, the steward quickly disappeared into his little room. We never did see him again, but I made sure he was listening. I talked loud enough. So this young fellow received the Baptism in the Holy Spirit.

After we landed, the pastor who was picking me up in Tulsa heard us speaking in tongues as we were coming down the aisle. He said, "That must be Dave." This is how we need to live and move and have our being. Most of us just aren't that confident in the Holy Spirit. We need to learn to lay our selves aside and let Him take over.

Ignorance Is Expensive!

The anointing is the love of Jesus. God's love is powerful! He says, "I love you!"

What you're reading here can change your life! All you need is one nugget and it's worth it all. It's time to practice using and sharing the revelation you already have. You've sat under the teaching of the Word and soaked in revelation knowledge for years. Now is the time to do something with what you've been given.

Many Christians don't understand the New Testament realities concerning the death, burial, and resurrection of the Lord Jesus Christ. What they're experiencing is much different than what He's given. How about you? What are you experiencing?

Ignorance is expensive. The more revelation you get, the greater you can enter into that fullness that Jesus promised. He said, **"I have come that they may have life, and that they may have *it* more abundantly."** The *New Living Translation* says, **"My purpose is to give life in all its fullness"** (John 10:10). I don't know about you, but I want to experience fullness. I don't want to experience just a little. I don't want to experience just forgiveness of sins. I want to experience being baptized in the Holy Ghost, walking in the Spirit, and functioning in the gifts of the Holy Spirit.

The Holy Ghost will talk to you. He's not just a religious Holy Spirit. He'll even tell you how to eat your hot dog! My friend loaded up his hot dog and was ready to eat it. The Holy Spirit said, "You'd better turn it around and bite into it from the other side." He didn't listen, but bit into it anyway. Mustard squirted everywhere! You say, "Ah, the Holy Ghost wouldn't tell you that!" Yes, He would—if you're listening.

How many times has He talked to you in that quiet voice saying, "Take your camera" or "Go back and get something" and you've reasoned, "Oh, I won't need that today." Then, the first thing you come to you lament, "Oh, I wish I had that!" That's how the Holy Spirit talks to us. If He spoke to us in a loud voice, we'd die.

A Major Collision

A friend of mine wanted to hear God speak. He prayed, "Oh Lord, speak to me. Please, speak to me." Not long after that he was taking his morning shower, when out of the top corner of the stall, God said, "Good morning, Jim." He immediately passed out right there in the shower. It's a miracle he didn't drown! We just need to practice listening for His still, small voice.

I asked the Holy Spirit one day, "How do You act, anyway?" He answered, "Just like you!" How does He act in Don Francisco? Like Don Francisco. We are the sum total of Jesus Himself. It would be boring if we were all the same. That's why God put me together with Andrew Wommack. We're so opposite it's scary! But we've been friends for all these years. When we minister together, it's show and tell, and tell and show. We've ministered that way for a long time.

We were at this big church up in Michigan. I was preaching on healing, and God gave me a word of knowledge. So I said, "Where's the person with rheumatoid arthritis?" A little grandma stood up slowly and started making her way up to the front. It took her five minutes to get there, so I had to keep on preaching. Finally, she arrived up front and looked up at me. I was on a tall platform looking down on this lady. I got so excited that I jumped off of the platform. In my excitement, I leaped wrong. Grandma and I were going to have a major collision!

Grandma looked up at me like a cat about to be run over by an eighteen-wheeler. Since I didn't have air brakes, I couldn't stop. So I body blocked grandma and we began to roll around on the floor. I wish I could tell you that my first thought was, *She's healed*, but my mind wasn't that renewed yet. Instead, I saw newspaper headlines, saying, "Healing Evangelist Kills Old Lady in Healing Line" and "Lawsuit!" Then, finally, I thought, *Oh God, please let me end up on top.* But she ended up laying nose to nose on top of me.

I opened my eyes and there she was. I see her about three times a year when I wake up in the middle of the night. I open my eyes, and there's grandma. She leaped off of me, grabbed that walker, held it over her head, and ran around that church. Glory to God! I walked back to the platform saying, "Thank You, Jesus!" That's going to be one of Heaven's Funniest Home Videos. When you get to heaven, you can go and check out that meeting.-

Make It An Adventure!

In fact, you can check yourself out in the meetings you've attended. You can see yourself listening to the preacher and thinking, *I don't believe that.* You'll see what you're thinking right up on the screen. So be happy, the camera is on you!

I can't wait to see Moses split the Red Sea. It'll be awesome to hear the rushing water in surround sound. We'll see his "great" faith. Really, he was saying, "HELP! GOD! HELP!" Read the Book. Moses was yelling to God. The Israelites saw a cloud of dust behind them, and it wasn't the Lone Ranger. You'll hear God say, "The rod, Moses. The rod."

Then the camera will be right on Moses as he says, "Boy, I hope this works!" Then we'll see the look of shock and awe on his face as the water parts. The whole time he's had his back to the crowd, so they don't know what's going on. Then he says, "Thank You, God!" and turns around to the people with confidence and authority, saying, "Go!" You watch, we'll see all this on video someday in living color!

We are complete in Christ. Once you renew your mind to this truth, it'll stop a lot of worry. God told me one day, "Worry is blasphemy against My promises." So I got smart, and hired a worrier—someone to worry for me. When I hired him, he asked me, "What do you pay?" I told him, "That's your first worry."

You need to laugh at challenging circumstances and problems. Just make an adventure out of it, saying, "Lord, I don't know how You're going to get me out of this one, but it's sure going to be awesome!" Hallelujah!

You Qualify!

If you can't have fun with Jesus, you're in religion! You become like who you hang around with. The Lord is telling the leaders in the body of Christ to lighten up!

Jesus was the happiest Man on earth (Heb. 1:9). I bet He short-sheeted His disciples' beds, played Hide & Seek with them, and threw them in the lake on occasion. When He healed somebody, do you think He cried? No! Jesus didn't say, "I'm sorry, devil. I'll take it easy on you next time." It would have been fun to travel with Jesus!

Religion paints a weak, boring picture of our Lord. "Oh, here comes Jesus walking along the shore of the Sea of Galilee. Right behind him—waddling in single file—are His twelve little ducks. Holy, holy, holy!" That's the picture painted for us in many churches.

However, I bet the disciples were half a mile ahead of Him, yelling, "See that Man down there? Bring the blind, bring the lame, bring the dumb. That guy can do anything!" That's what they were doing.

Jesus knew who He was. He knew His calling. He came to do good and deliver people. He said, "If you've seen Me, you've seen My Father."

Be Yourself!

That's our job! We're here to reveal to people what Jesus is really like—and God uses all the gifts. The Father gave gifts to the Church, Jesus gave gifts to the Church, and the Holy Spirit gave gifts to the Church. They're all Givers! Jesus gave apostles, prophets, evangelists, pastors, and teachers. We all operate different. Every office functions in a different manner.

Andrew Wommack is a teacher. To him, the Word is power. The Word comes forth and sets people free. You don't have to minister like he does, or I do. We're all different personalities. God works differently through each one of us. You need to find out what your calling is. People ask me, "Why do you make all those noises when you pray for people?" I want to. I like it. I enjoy hearing myself go PPSSTT and BLAM! Hey, if I don't enjoy my ministry, you won't either. I enjoy my job! I like ministering to people. It's fun to sneak up behind someone and release the anointing. There's just something inside of me that likes to do that.

When I travel and the pastor is late picking me up at the airport, I hide from them. They're running around saying, "Where is he?" and I'm hiding behind some post. I just like to see them think, *I missed him!* I don't know where that comes from. I'm sixty-seven, but I'm a kid at heart. I just like to have fun and make an adventure out of everything. I'm just not the stoic type, I guess. God had to find me out on a ranch. It's just how the Lord has called, anointed, and gifted me. Just be yourself!

Learning His Identity

We are complete in Him. God has given us everything we need. He hasn't held anything back. We have everything Jesus had. It's the same Holy Spirit living on the inside of us. Jesus had to find out who He was. When do you think He discovered His identity? Did He just wake up one day and say, "Wow, I'm the Messiah!"? Of course not! He was taught. He had to learn these things. Once He had understanding, His mother sat Him down and said, "Hey Jesus. Let me tell You Your story. Joseph is not Your Father."

"What?"

"No, he wasn't. A big old angel showed up to me, and because I believed, You came. Your name is Jesus. I was going to name my first son 'Paul,' but You're Jesus. You're the Messiah. You're the One we've been looking for."

"Really?" I bet his little brain went WHIRR.

I read a book that they had found in the old synagogues. It was like a reporter recorded when Jesus was walking on earth. They said Joseph was a very ugly man. He had no personality. That's what the book said. Even his own family didn't think that Jesus was going to amount to anything. But here's an interesting fact: Jesus spent a lot of time with a prophet who lived down the road. Do you know what that tells me? That prophet was schooling Jesus in who He was.

He had to believe His identity just like you and me. He had to believe what the Word said about Him. Jesus never heard His Father speak until He walked into the river. But He had the Holy Spirit. At age twelve, He was already debating with the religious leaders. Jesus already knew who He was at age twelve! For those first thirty years, He found out His identity and learned how to walk on the face of this earth.

Then—just as soon as He blew out His thirtieth candle—Jesus looked at His mother and said, "I'm out of here! There's a wild man down at the river waiting for Me. I have a divine appointment in the middle of the water."

"Behold, the Lamb"

In the Old Testament, when a family picked out a lamb to sacrifice, it became the family pet. It lived in the house and the children became attached to it. But when the time came, they brought this lamb—a perfect lamb—to the priest. Then the priest examined the lamb—not the family. He looked at the lamb and said, "This will do." Then the entire family watched the priest slit that lamb's throat and chop it up to offer as a sacrifice for their sin. This was quite an event!

This is an awesome type and shadow of what Jesus did!

Back at the river, John the Baptist was preaching. I don't know why people went to listen to him speak. How would you like to hear: "You snakes! You vipers! Who has warned you of the wrath to come? You slither down here like serpents trying to change your snake skins in the water." The people said, "Boy, that's good preaching!"

I hear that in the Church today. Listen to some of these preachers on radio or television. They're beating people up. They're working them over, mentioning every sin in the Book. "If you have one of these, then you need to respond!" Sure fills the altars up with people.

Anyway, here's John standing in the river delivering one of these scathing sermons. Then, all at once, he looks up and says, "Behold, the Lamb of God who takes away the sins of the world." That was revelation knowledge! The Holy Ghost spoke through him when he saw the Lord.

Jesus walked into the water and said, "Alright, go ahead and do your thing." John put Him under, and the Holy Spirit descended upon Him when He came back up. Then Jesus heard His Father for the first time, saying, "This is My beloved Son, in whom I am well pleased." He hadn't done one miracle yet, but the Father was pleased. That's awesome!

"Stay Hidden!"

Then the Spirit of God drove Jesus into the wilderness to be tempted of the devil. This was very important. Why did the Holy Spirit do this? Because we finally have a Man on the earth who knows who He is. Jesus was going to reverse all things. He fasted. Then the devil showed up and tempted Him just like he tempts all of us.

Right away, the enemy tried to get Jesus into works. "If you are the Son of God, change these stones into bread." Boldly, the Lord answered, "It is written." In other words, Jesus said, "I don't have to prove that I'm the Son of God. I know I am. I just heard My Father say it, and I don't have to prove it to you!"

We get the same temptation! As soon as we're born again, the devil tries to get us into doing good works in order to please God when the truth is we're already accepted. When you were born again, you became as righteous as you're ever going to be. Righteousness was given to you as a free gift.

So guess what we've been doing most of our lives? Trying to prove our identity to God. If we function good, God loves us. If we don't, He doesn't love us. Although that's the way we grew up, it's the wrong message!

That's why this message—God has accepted us—is so freeing. We were taught that God looked us over and saw how much sin we had. I have news for you. God didn't even examine you. He looked at the sacrifice. He examined the Lamb. God didn't even look at us! He looked at Jesus. We got in by believing. All God heard was our voice. That's why it's so hard for people to accept this. We have nothing to do with it!

The Father, Son, and Holy Spirit got together in heaven and had a little committee meeting. They said, "If We're going to save this bunch on earth, We're going to have to do it Ourselves." And that's exactly what They did. Jesus came down here and did it all. Isn't that awesome?

We are hidden in Christ. I say, "Stay hidden!" Don't come out and say, "Here I am!" Let God be God and stay in Him. Hallelujah!

"Sin Too Much"

While ministering up in Canada, I saw this whole row of guys with the same type shirt on sitting in the back day after day. Finally, about the third morning, I asked the biggest fellow in the bunch, "Who are you?" He was just about as big as Dave Hinton. With thick, muscular arms, legs like tree trunks, and tattoos everywhere, he looked like he could kick start a 747. I called him up to the front and asked, "What are you guys doing here?"

He answered, "We work for that man right back there. He owns the electric company. He gave us a choice. We could either go to work or come here and listen to you. Since we didn't want to work, we came to hear you." This was one honest fellow.

So I asked him, "Are you born again? Are you a Christian?"

"Nope. Sin too much."

"Congratulations—that's what qualifies you for salvation! If you wouldn't have sinned, Jesus wouldn't have had to die. If you've sinned a bunch, then you qualify a bunch."

He started to get it. "You mean that my sin qualifies me for getting saved?"

"Yeah!"

"I can believe that." And he got saved right there. Then he said, "I've been watching you back there. You've been kicking the feet out from under the people. When they fall, it's because you knocked their feet out from under them."

"Give It to Me!"

"Okay, you've challenged me. Now I'm going to challenge you." In my heart, I prayed, *Holy Spirit, give him the best shot You can give him.* I said, "I want no ushers, please. None." (They couldn't have caught him anyway.) I instructed him, "Brace yourself the best way you know how." As he did, I kept praying, *Lord, give it to him. If ever there's a time, it's now. If You've ever nailed someone, nail this guy!* Then I told him, "I'm going move my hand down your back like this (what I call "the Chop"), but I'm not going to touch you. We'll see what the Holy Spirit does." *Oh God, please!*

As I went down his back, it was like the Holy Spirit hit him with a two-by-four right behind his knees. His legs went straight out and there he was—prone—in midair. Then he landed—WHAM—flat on his back like a pancake! In my heart, I said, "YES!"

Down on the floor, he yelled, "It's real! It's real! It's real!" Then he jumped up and said, "Give it to me! Give me what you've got!"

"Do you want to be filled with the Holy Spirit?"

"Yes!"

I laid hands on him and—BOOM!—he hit the floor speaking in tongues. I told him, "Sit right there, brother. You're going to be my best audience. I could just visualize him going into a bar and saying, "Hey, do you want to hear about Jesus?"

That's God!

I led a big truck driver to the Lord once. He found somebody messing around with his girlfriend, and caught him at a truck stop. He pulled this guy off the truck and was just about ready to knock his lights out when Jesus asked, "What are you doing?"

He answered, "I'm going to knock his lights out."

"No you're not. Tell him about Me."

"Oh, okay." Then he asked this guy he had jacked up against this truck, "Hey, do you want to know about Jesus?"

And this fellow whimpered, "Yes. Yes, please!" You can't tell me that Jesus doesn't have a sense of humor. That's God!

"Those Who Believe"

We are complete in Him! We're loaded, gifted, and blessed! Lack makes you the center of every equation. Faith makes Jesus the center. Praise God! We're finding out more and more how God made us. We're made in His image.

Aren't you glad the Holy Spirit is our teacher? When I was first baptized in the Holy Ghost, I thought I was the only one in the country. I read in the Book, **"These signs will follow those who believe"** (Mark 16:17). It didn't say, "Only apostles, prophets, evangelists, pastors, and teachers…" The Word says, **"Those who believe."** Being the simple guy that I am, I just looked at my hands and declared, "I'm a believer. When I lay these hands on the sick, they shall recover!" What made me different than anybody else? I believed.

So I started laying hands on sick cows and horses—anything that moved. Then I began laying hands on people. I noticed such a change in my life. I had boldness to tell others about Jesus!

I led some Canadians to the Lord. Then I told them about the Baptism in the Holy Spirit. When I started talking about tongues, I thought this guy was going to jump right out of the pickup. He asked, "What's that? What's tongues?"

I answered, "It sounds like this…" and prayed in tongues.

He said, "I want that!"

"You do?"

God gave me a hungry guy! He received the Baptism in the Holy Spirit there in Arkansas at our other ranch. We spoke in tongues together all the way to the airport. There we were in the airport, speaking out loud to each other in our prayer languages!

Emphasis & Animation

My son-in-law and I go through airports praying back and forth in tongues together out loud. People just think we're from another country. They don't even pay attention to us!

Many people think that God is monotonous. They speak in tongues in this dry, dull, and boring manner. God's up there going, "What?" You wouldn't talk to your friend in monotone. Why do it to God? Put a little emphasis and animation into it! You're talking to the King of kings and Lord of lords, not some fencepost!

You can even be your own entertainment system. I drive down the road by myself modulating my voice—up and down, louder and softer, faster and slower—in tongues. It's not monotonous being a Spirit-filled Christian—it's exciting! We're born again and filled with the Holy Ghost. We're talking to the Almighty God who created us. I hope I'm changing your whole language system. Isn't that how you'd like to be talked to?

I've been all over the world and heard many different kinds of foreign languages—Swahili, French, even tonal dialects of Chinese. God created these languages. He enjoys them! How much more then should He enjoy it when we express ourselves with our heavenly language of tongues! We're loaded!

Release His Power

The Holy Spirit is our Teacher. He wants you to be stretched, so He'll often set you up.

I was invited to the Full Gospel Businessman's meeting just down the road in Fort Morgan, Colorado. All the way out there I was praying, "Oh, God, give me something to say. All I've done is lay hands on cows and horses. What am I going to tell them—Old Bessie got healed?" I didn't have much of a testimony.

Then the Holy Spirit told me, "Just say, 'The first man who stands up gets healed.'" I thought, *Oh, okay. No problem.* But give your mind three hours to think about it. You'll go through every excuse in the book. "Well, I wonder if they don't get healed. That'll be the end of my ministry—and I'm just getting started!" Finally, I just told my brain to "Shut up! Just do what the Holy Spirit said to do."

So when they introduced me, I stood up and said, "Hey, the first man who stands up gets healed!" Two guys shot up. I said, "Whoa!" and tried to size them up. I wanted to see what was wrong with them so I could pick the one who was least ill—as if that made any difference anyway.

So I asked the older gentleman, "Would you please come up here?" As he moved toward the front, I saw that his arms were locked in a ninety-degree angle, and his hands were crooked and gnarled from severe arthritis. I wanted to say, "King's X. Sit down" and then ask the other fellow, "What's wrong with you?" But it was too late. I was committed.

"What Is He Doing?"

Did you know that your anointing leaks out of your eyes? It's true! So I closed my eyes and told him, "Come on over here and give me your hands." When he stuck those gnarled old hands in mine, my mind screamed, "Aargh!" I could feel the crookedness, but I didn't know his shoulders were locked. He was locked up all over. All of a sudden, I felt him jerking me back and forth. I wondered, *What is he doing?* He thought, *What is he doing? Doesn't he know my shoulders don't work?* The Holy Spirit was jerking two jerks!

Back and forth, back and forth, back and forth we went. We worked ourselves up over my head before I was bold enough to open my eyes— and his fingers were perfect. He let out a huge scream and said, "Look at this! Look at this!" Then he ran around showing everybody. I was going, "Whoa!" I hadn't even said a word yet. The Holy Spirit is so smart!

The anointing was very strong. I started giving my testimony, but then said, "Hold it! The Holy Spirit tells me that there's somebody here with a heart problem. Where are you?" It was the young guy! I asked him, "What's wrong with you?"

He answered, "I worked for the power company. I got hit by lightning on a power post. I was dead on the post, but when I hit the ground, the impact from the fall shook my heart and got it started again but the doctors say I'll never be able to work again." He was twenty-one years old.

"Get out there in the aisle." And I shot him with the power. That was the first time I ever shot anybody!

"Keep Practicing!"

Just act like you know what you're doing. Go home and faint later. Don't say, "My God, his eyes opened!" Go home and do that. Bluff your way through. That's what the devil does. You have to act like you know what you're doing. If nothing happens, say, "Just practicing."

I was in the Philippines with 600 pastors underneath a shed. Half of them were on one side, and half on the other. We were hot and sweaty, and had this big old fan blowing on us. I told my friend who was with me, "Watch this." I picked up that fan, pointed it at half the group, and blew into it. Three hundred people fell out under the power.

He went, "Whoa, let me try!"

"Okay, this other side is yours." He blew and about ten guys fell out. I told him, "It comes with practice, brother. Just keep practicing!" You're loaded!

"Raw Faith"

This young guy in Fort Morgan hit the floor. I asked, "Does anybody here know how to listen to hearts?"

This one fellow said, "I don't, but I'm willing to try." He got down there, listened, and declared, "Sounds good to me!"

This young guy went back to the doctor on Monday, and they examined him all week long. Finally, they concluded, "You didn't get a repaired heart. You got a brand-new one!" That was what I call "raw faith." I didn't know what I was doing!

You can exercise yourself right out of faith. You can also educate yourself out of faith. How many Christians have you heard say, "I used to do that"? Many people come to my meetings and say, "This is the way it used to be!" I preached a meeting in Smith Wigglesworth's church. We had one of those runaway meetings. I heard later that the people commented, "We haven't had a meeting like this since Smith Wigglesworth!" Why not? It's the same Holy Spirit. He wants to demonstrate. He desires to work on the people. We just have to learn to lay our selves aside and go for it!

"Straight Hair?"

We didn't know anything about devils. We never heard anything about them in our church. We were probably loaded with them, but we never heard about it. So after I was baptized in the Holy Spirit, I didn't want a deliverance ministry.

But one day I was talking with this nice looking Presbyterian lady. She said, "I think I have a devil."

"You do?" I had heard that you're supposed to get their names. So I told her, "I've never done this before, but I'll be talking to the devil. So don't listen to what I'm saying." I said, "What's your name in Jesus' name?" Nothing. I thought it was the way I said it. So I lowered my voice an octave or two and repeated, "What's your name in Jesus' name?" Then I tried going several octaves higher saying, "What's your name in Jesus' name?" I worked on this lady for fifteen minutes!

Finally, a little voice came out of her mouth. "Straight hair."

I said, "What?" The hair on the back of my neck stood straight up. I thought she was going to say, "murder" or something like that. I said, "Straight hair? What do you do?"

"She gets a permanent and I make it straight."

"What do you do that for?"

"Well, she gets mad at herself and so does her husband. That's my job!"

"Mi Casa!"

Thank God He gave me a straight hair devil. I shouted, "You straight hair devil, come out of her!" It came out.

64

A week later, she came to our house on a Sunday afternoon to show off her curls. "Look at this! My permanent has stuck for a week!"

I asked this devil once, "What's your name?"

He answered, "Liar."

"Are you telling me the truth?"

One morning at 2:00, our doorbell rang. I tried to find my bathrobe without turning the light on. While groping around in the closet, my hand brushed against this little soft thing. It was my wife's pink one. I thought, *That'll work. This guy is probably lost and wants directions.* So I put on my wife's little pink robe, walked to the door, and opened it. Wide-eyed, this guy looked at me and cleared his throat. I asked, "May I help you?"

He said, "Are you the guy who casts out devils?"

I answered, "Yes, sir. You got one?"

"Yes, sir."

"Then come on in."

That devil said, "Mi casa. Mi casa!" I knew enough Spanish to know he was saying, "My house."

I told him, "It's not your house. Out!"

Stupid Devils

I'd just married this young couple a few months earlier. The lady called me and said, "Pastor, get over here right away! There's something wrong with my husband!"

That's the way we were taught. So guess what pastors do? They put the flashing red light on their head and run right to the emergency.

When I arrived at their garden level apartment, she opened the door all flustered saying, "Oh Pastor, come in here. Come in here!"

When I looked at him, I thought I was going to see a dead man or something. He was just sitting there in the chair. So I asked him, "What's wrong?"

He answered, "My name is Eckar. I am of Legion and we are many."

Most Christians would have said, "What was that name? Eckar?" But something hit me and I got funny. I walked over to the guy and laughed at him, saying, "You stupid devils! Don't you know Jesus defeated you at the cross?"

"Yeah, I know that, but we win in the end."

"No, you don't! I read the back of the Book and your future looks terrible."

"Spirit of Might"

He got up and walked to the other side of the room. So I decided to sit down where he sat. No use both of us standing. Then all at once I felt something welling up on the inside. I thought, *What's this? Am I getting possessed of the devil or what?* This thing was stirring on the inside of me. Then I heard the Holy Spirit say, "Spirit of Might, son. Spirit of Might."

Jesus had this Spirit (Is. 11:2). I believe that's how the prophet outran the king's chariot (1 Kin. 18:46). The Spirit of Might came on him. I'd never been in a position where I needed a Spirit of Might before, but I felt a supernatural inner strength mounting. I thought to myself, *My God, I'm turning into the Incredible Hulk!* Do you know what I heard the Holy Spirit say? "Act like the Hulk!"

So I started making all these Incredible Hulk noises and this guy was getting concerned. On the inside, I was laughing and saying, "I wish I had a video of this!" He was trying to climb the walls and get away from me, but he kept sliding down.

We think of Samson like he was this buff, muscle-bound, hunk of a man lifting weights every day. We picture him as Mr. Bodybuilder himself. No! He probably looked like any other average guy. The Word says, "The Spirit of the Lord came upon him," not "his big muscles showed up." The same Spirit of the Lord came upon me with might. I tell you, I was so strong!

I could have picked that kid up and thrown him across the room and through the window, but God didn't send me to kill him. I just touched him and he flew way back across the floor. His glasses fell off and he got a rug burn across his nose. He laid there like a dead man for quite some time.

"Two Live Ones"

Finally, his wife eased over by me and asked, "Is he dead?"

I answered, "No, God didn't kill him."

Pretty soon, he woke up. I started questioning him. He said he felt like he fell into a sewer hole. He'd gotten depressed, and then possessed. He felt them enter his body from his feet up. He heard lots of voices inside. Do you know what the main voice said? "We've been sent here by satan himself to kill Dave Duell." Do you know what that told me? If you need a Spirit of Might, you got it. Whatever you need is on the inside of you!

We have nothing to worry about. The devil is under our feet. We're the ones who have authority. He works through ignorance and fear.

The first time I ran into this was in St. Louis. We went to a Christian businessman's meeting. We flew out there in a little airplane. I was telling my friend about the Holy Spirit. He wanted to receive the Baptism. We looked in the yellow pages for where to go. I saw Teen Challenge, and said, "These people believe in that. I read their book. We can go there." So we took a taxi over to Teen Challenge.

There we were—a couple of country boys. We walked in and I said, "I'm filled with the Spirit, but this guy (pointing to my friend) wants to be."

The skinny little pastor sitting behind a metal desk said, "So you guys want to be filled with the Spirit?" He got that silly little grin on his face that said, "I've got two live ones here!"

When that guy laid hands on me it was like Samson hit me. My friend received the Baptism in the Holy Spirit, and I just lay on the floor speaking away in tongues. We were so jazzed up and filled with the Spirit that we felt like we could do anything!

Ignorance

We went back to the hotel to tell our friend who had flown in with us. He was a bodybuilder—always had every hair in place, perfect. We were in the big hotel ballroom telling him about how my friend got filled with the Spirit. All at once, something happened. This bodybuilder got down on his hands and knees, and ran around that place laughing like crazy. Then all at once he stood up and it was obvious that someone else was in there. He looked at me and said, "I am not Leonard. My name is Jesus."

I thought, *No, you're not Jesus!* and launched into emergency tongues.

He looked at my friend who had just received the Holy Spirit and said, "Don't say a word. If you say a word, you'll just drop over dead." You could have stuck a crowbar in Don's mouth and not gotten anything out. He looked back at me and said, "Don't close your eyes, Dave. If you close your eyes, you're going to die!" Now he has my friend shut up and me trying to keep my eyes open. I'm scared to death and don't know what to do. I'd never been in that position before in my life!

However, the demon had forgotten about the older gentleman from New York who was also in the room. He walked in between Don and me, grabbed Leonard by the ears, and cast the devil out of him. My knees were knocking. Leonard woke up and said, "What's wrong with you guys? What's going on here?"

"You don't know? A demon was in you!"

"What? No way! There was no demon in me."

Leonard slept in the same room as Don and me. So for the rest of that trip, we took turns watching him at night. That's ignorance. We were ignorant. We didn't know we had authority.

Ask Him to Teach You

You need to know who you are, what God has given you, and how to use it. The devil uses ignorance. However, once you discover what God has given you, you can walk around like Jesus. That's what He wants us to do—every one of us! God doesn't just want this for one or two believers here and there. Every one of us is loaded!

One day, the Lord told me, "You'll never see My bigness manifested until you allow yourself to get into a position where I can show Myself mighty." We're all chickens—we like to play it safe. Let's get out there where God can show Himself mighty and manifest Himself through us. He will because we're loaded. He's put everything we need—Himself—on the inside of us.

Someone recently asked, "How do you release the anointing?" Easy. The power source is in your spirit man—your belly. When the turbo charger kicks in, just let that power run through your arms (or wherever you want it to go) and then stick it in your hand. So many people are loaded, but don't know how to release it. It's like pitching a baseball—wind up and let it go! (For more about this, check out my teaching called *"How to Flow in the Supernatural."*)

I watched a karate championship awhile back. It was just individuals—one person—doing their thing. They were hollering, yelling, and moving their hands to direct their power a certain way. I thought, *If the devil does that, then what about us?* I know we don't have to be quite that demonstrative, but I enjoy it.

We need to learn how to release the power of God within us. I believe that when I make certain noises while I'm ministering, it releases something. That's just how the Holy Spirit taught me. You need to ask Him to teach you—then step out in faith and go for it!

"Release Them!"

Jesus said, "Heal the sick," not "Pray for the sick." I don't even pray for the sick anymore. I just release the power to heal. The shorter the prayer, the greater the faith. Sometimes I just issue the command, "Be

69

healed!" and then release the power into them. When you're ministering in front of a group, you need to constantly be on the lookout for people who are really receptive. They'll make you look good!

I'm the total opposite of Benny Hinn. He'd say, "Don't make a noise. Don't anybody move. No one go to the bathroom. We don't want to upset the Holy Spirit." That's just the way He works in him. Let Benny be Benny. With me, if you have to go to the bathroom, please go!

I heard Pastor Cho in Virginia Beach at a big Assembly of God church. My seat was way up in the balcony. Pastor Cho came out and in his thick Korean accent said, "This afternoon, Holy Spirit show me big problem. Big problem in this meeting tonight. Big problem!" I was thinking, *My goodness, somebody must have cancer or something.* "Big problem in this meeting tonight." He kept working it and working it. I wanted to know what the problem was!

Finally, he said, "Constipation. Constipation! Release them, Lord—release them!" At least 150 people stood up in a panic and ran for the door. I laughed so hard! All I could think of was the toilets. What would they do when there wasn't enough?

I told this story at one of our conferences. When I got to the part where he said, "Release them, Lord—release them!" about twenty-five people stood up and ran for the door. It even works in a joke!

We're loaded! But if we don't release God's power, the people won't get it!

How You Can Receive Jesus and His Holy Spirit

No matter who you are…
No matter where you are…
You matter to God!

Not because of what you do…
Nor what you've ever done…
God loves you because—God is Love!

"This is love: not that we loved God, but that He loved us and sent His Son as an atoning sacrifice for our sins" (adapted from 1 John 4:10).

"For God so loved the world that He gave His only begotten Son, that whoever believes in Him should not perish but have everlasting life" (John 3:16).

Jesus Loves You!

"As the Father loved Me, I also have loved you; abide in My love" (John 15:9).

"Greater love has no one than this, than to lay down one's life for his friends." Jesus said, "You are My friends" (John 15:13-14).

Jesus has done all the work for you!

The work is finished. Jesus did His part. All you need to do is act on it and receive it.

"If you confess with your mouth the Lord Jesus and believe in your heart that God has raised Him from the dead, you will be saved. For with the heart one believes unto righteousness, and with the mouth confession is made unto salvation"
(Romans 10:9-10).

Choose God's love!

Pray this prayer from your heart…

Father, in Jesus' name, I confess with my mouth that Jesus is Lord. I believe with my heart that God raised Him from the dead. Jesus, I ask You right now to come live in me. I receive You.
I repent for all my sin; I receive forgiveness, and I am now a new creature in Jesus Christ.
Thank You, Jesus!

Congratulations! You are now in Christ…

A Brand-New Creature
"Therefore, if anyone *is* in Christ, *he is* a new creation; old things have passed away; behold, all things have become new"
(2 Corinthians 5:17).

Righteous…In Right-Standing With God
"For He made Him who knew no sin *to be* sin for us, that we might become the righteousness of God in Him"
(2 Corinthians 5:21).

Free from Condemnation
"*There is* therefore now no condemnation to those who are in Christ Jesus" (Romans 8:1).

Healed—Body, Soul, and Spirit
Jesus "Himself bore our sins in His own body on the tree, that we, having died to sins, might live for righteousness—by whose stripes (wounds) you were healed" (1 Peter 2:24).

Free from Fear
"For God has not given us a spirit of fear, but of power and of love and of a sound mind"
(2 Timothy 1:7).

Free from Poverty
"I have come that they may have life, and that they may have *it* more abundantly"
(John 10:10).

Now that you are a believer in Jesus Christ, He wants to fill you with His Holy Spirit.
"But you shall be baptized with the Holy Spirit" (Acts 1:5).

The Holy Spirit comes to you as a gift from Jesus.
"You shall receive the gift of the Holy Spirit" (Acts 2:38).

The Holy Spirit gives you power to live your new life.
"But you shall receive power when the Holy Spirit has come upon you" (Acts 1:8).

The Holy Spirit gives you a heavenly language.
"And they were all filled with the Holy Spirit and began to speak with other tongues, as the Spirit gave them utterance" (Acts 2:4).

Speaking in your heavenly language builds you up in your faith.
"He who speaks in a tongue edifies himself" (1 Corinthians 14:4).
"But you, beloved, building yourselves up on your most holy faith, praying in the Holy Spirit" (Jude 20).

Your mind will not understand because it is your spirit praying.
For if I pray in a tongue, my spirit prays, but my understanding is unfruitful" (1 Corinthians 14:14).

Out of your heart will flow rivers of living water.
"'He who believes in Me, as the Scripture has said, out of his heart (belly) will flow rivers of living water.' But this He spoke concerning the Holy Spirit, whom those believing in Him would receive" (John 7:38-39).

Every believer who asks for the Holy Spirit in faith receives Him.
"How much more will *your* heavenly Father give the Holy Spirit to those who ask Him!" (Luke 11:13).

Let's pray right now:
Father, I am thirsty. I'm hungry. Baptize me with Your Holy Spirit.
Fill me with Your power.
I receive it now, in Jesus' name. Thank You, Father! Praise You, Jesus!

You have just received the Holy Spirit by faith. It is important to act on that faith by giving voice. Allow those unfamiliar syllables and words rising up out of your belly (where your spirit is) to come out of your mouth. Yield your tongue to Him by speaking aloud your new heavenly language. The Holy Spirit is giving your spirit these words in order to pray the perfect will of God for you. Isn't that awesome! You have been baptized in the Holy Spirit!

You can choose to pray in your new tongue anytime, anywhere, and as much as you want from now on for the rest of your life! The more you pray in the Spirit, the more you build yourself up in your faith supernaturally.

The power of God will help you to live your new life in Christ. He will give you the desire and ability to tell many other people what Jesus has done for you. Be bold because He is with you!

Two Tips for Getting Started in Your New Life

Read your Bible every day.
We recommend starting in the New Testament and concentrating on the Gospels at first (Matthew, Mark, Luke, and John) because they focus most directly upon the life and teachings of Jesus Christ. If you miss a day, no need to feel condemned. Just start back up again!

Find a group of believers who love Jesus and encourage the Holy Spirit to move in their midst.
Jesus wants you to grow up in your faith while being connected to other believers through meaningful relationships.

Congratulations and welcome to God's family!
You now have millions of brothers and sisters in Christ all around the world.

If you prayed either one or both of these prayers today, please contact us so that we can rejoice with you!

Faith Ministries
P.O. Box 609
Littleton, CO 80160
(303) 777-1113
www.fmin.org

About the Author

Dave Duell grew up on a farm in Kersey, Colorado. The youngest of thirteen children, Dave learned many of life's valuable lessons through hard work and love. His strict father taught him discipline and his gentle mother taught him love. Dave says, "The training I received growing up on a large farm let me see how God operates through many practical experiences."

Two specific incidents influenced Dave in his early years to bring him to where he is today. One event happened when he was twelve years old. He spent a week at a Bible camp in the Rocky Mountains of Colorado and heard the testimony of a missionary from the Congo of Africa. That week Dave accepted Jesus into his life and from then on had a heart for missions. The other event happened when he was fifteen years old. One day by a hay bale out in the field, Dave knelt down and asked God for the privilege of being wealthy enough to support five hundred missionaries. This prayer has stayed vivid in his mind and influenced his life to this very day.

Later, when he graduated from high school, he chose to go to North Park Junior College in Chicago, Illinois, to put some distance between himself and the farm chores and to find a wife! God answered his prayers and he met and later married Bonnie McCartney from Chicago, Illinois. He brought her home to live on the ranch in Kersey, Colorado.

God blessed them with three lovely daughters, Tamara, Juli, and Darla. Later they adopted a beautiful little Korean girl and named her Sarah. As Dave and Bonnie raised their girls, they taught them the love of Jesus and were very involved in their church.

When Dave was thirty-one years old, his desire to know the Holy Spirit personally began to increase. One night he was invited to a Full Gospel Businessmen's meeting in Denver, Colorado. That night he asked for the Baptism in the Holy Spirit and the power of God actually came into his life. It was the beginning of many adventures!

You can read more of this story in Dave's two autobiographical books: ***Faith Believe It... or Not*** and ***Faith, What A Deal!*** (See the Additional Resources Available pages)

Dave and Bonnie maintained their cattle ranch, but also began testifying everywhere about the love and power of Jesus. During these years of following God, they learned to release miracles to others, bring deliverance to those in bondage, and walk in the joy of the Lord. They eventually began Bible studies in a home, which by 1978 evolved into a church in Greeley, Colorado. Years before, the Lord had spoken to Dave, "I am giving you a ministry called 'Faith Ministries,'" thus the new church was named Faith Ministries Fellowship.

Their international ministry began in 1980, when Dave and Bonnie took a team from their church to Kenya, East Africa. It was the beginning of many trips and crusades around the world.

Dave and Bonnie served as senior pastors of this growing congregation until 1992 when they were called by God to start another Faith Ministries church in Denver, Colorado. Now this congregation is touching the Denver area and the world with the love and joy of Jesus. It's called Faith Ministries Church International.

Today, Dave and Bonnie's family has grown to include sons-in-law, many grandchildren, and a great-grandson. Their spiritual family has grown to include many nations.

Dave and Bonnie have traveled to seventy-three nations bringing healing, encouragement, and joy. Over and over they find themselves being spiritual parents to pastors and ministry leaders that they meet everywhere they go.

In 1998, God re-birthed a desire in Dave and Bonnie to join together with others in the Body of Christ and form a network that could pool the resources of its partners and facilitate the advancement of the Kingdom of God beyond the ability of a single person, ministry, or church. They began by forming an Apostolic Team as an extension of their anointing and ministry. This team is available to the network partners for training, encouragement, counsel, and resource referral.

Today, FMIN has grown to over one-hundred-ninety partners,

representing hundreds of churches, ministries, and businesses in thirty-three countries. (For more information, please see the FMIN pages in this book)

Dave and Bonnie would like to extend to you a warm invitation to join them for fellowship sometime when you are in the Denver area or at one of the many worldwide events and conferences sponsored by Faith Ministries. Please visit www.daveduell.com, www.fmin.org, or www. faithministries.ws for current information.

Additional Resources from Dave and Bonnie Duell

Books

Faith, Believe It Or Not by Dave Duell

The first of two fast moving autobiographical books, FBION was written to show you how you can experience Jesus in a real and exciting way for yourself. Through his own personal journey to practice and imitate Jesus, Dave shares the joy and wonder of the simplicity of Christianity. While reading this book, many people have stayed up late at night crying and praising God!

Faith, What A Deal! by Dave Duell

This second installment continues the story from part one above. You will be inspired to live in a higher dimension of faith. Through personal experience and the Word of God, Dave shares what God has done for us through Jesus Christ. By the end of the book you will ultimately say with him… "Faith, what a deal!" (Warning: Only read this book if you want to be stirred to the core of your being!)

How to Flow in the Supernatural by Dave Duell

Have you desired to see God's supernatural power flow to you and through you more effectively? Dave illustrates this illuminating study of the anointing with personal stories and actual testimonies that will stir your faith for greater manifestations of the Holy Spirit in your life!

Throw Yourself A Party by Dave Duell

How do you react when things don't go your way? What do you do when everything seems to go wrong? In this insightful book, you'll learn biblical principles for dealing with these types of difficult situations. As you discover these living truths from God's Word, you'll be refreshed in your spirit and set on a new course of victory over life's challenges! Go ahead—throw yourself a party!

Knowing God by Dave Duell

Your relationship with God is the most important thing in your life! Jesus has done everything necessary for you to be able to walk, talk, and listen to Him on a daily basis. The miracles will inspire you and the insights from God's Word concerning righteousness will ground you for your own intimate and supernatural walk with the Lord. Life is truly found in "Knowing God!"

Audio Messages

How to Flow in the Anointing
Dave Duell gives practical application to an important scriptural topic. Laced with humor and personal stories, you'll be challenged to enjoy the simplicity of God's anointing. (4 CDs)

Knowing God
Knowing God is not a mystery! Learn how to have a loving relationship with Him in this series by Dave Duell. (4 CDs)

Do You Know Who You Are?
Find out who you really are in Jesus Christ! Dave Duell shares in this audio series. (4 CDs)

Walking by Faith
A Faith Ministries trademark! Dave Duell uncovers the joy and simplicity of believing God. (2 CDs)

Awake to Righteousness
Dave Duell wonderfully describes what took place for you during Jesus' death, burial, and resurrection. This message can change your life forever! (2 CDs)

Merry Heart
A Duell classic! In these exciting, hilarious messages, Dave describes his early days being baptized in the Holy Spirit and getting started in the miracle ministry. If you are new to Dave, this is a great series in which to get better acquainted! (2 CDs)

Marking Your Children for God
Bonnie Duell equips you to guide your children as arrows to hit the target God has for them. Bonnie, wife of Dave Duell, mother of four daughters, grandmother of eighteen grandchildren, great-grandmother of seven

great-grandchildren, and partner with the Holy Spirit, is an authority in this area. (2 CDs)

Women of Excellence
Taught by a woman of excellence, Bonnie Duell shares practical insights on God's view of women in this audio series. (2 CDs)

God's Will In Your Home
Dave and Bonnie work together to teach this series of inspiring messages on the will of God for your household. They give much needed encouragement, direction, and support in identifying with God's plan for your marriage and family. (2 CDs)

Complete listings of products from the Duells, along with many FREE audio messages, are available at **www.fmin.org** We invite you to shop our online store!

To place an order or request a full catalog of the Duells' books, videos, and CDs, please contact us at:

Dave Duell Ministries
P.O. Box 609
Littleton, CO 80160
USA

Phone: (303) 777-1113
Fax: (303) 777-9342
Email: info@fmin.org
Website: www.fmin.org
Radio: "Walk By Faith" Mon-Fri, 6:15pm
KLT AM 670 in the Metro-Denver area
Free audio podcasts available at the iTunes Store

Faith Ministries International Network

"Joining together to expand the Kingdom of God"

FMIN is a relational network of independent churches and ministries under the spiritual guidance of Dave and Bonnie Duell and Dennis and Denise Capra. Our message is the freedom of grace and peace through faith righteousness in Jesus Christ.

FMIN Founders

Dave and Bonnie Duell serve as the founding leaders of Faith Ministries International Network. Their local church, Faith Ministries Church International (Denver, Colorado, USA), is a partnering ministry in FMIN. They serve on the Apostolic Leadership Team with Dennis and Denise Capra (Co-pastors of Faith Ministries World Outreach Center, Kansas City, Missouri, USA).

What Is FMIN?

In 1998, God re-birthed a desire in Dave and Bonnie to join together with other leaders in the Body of Christ and form a relational network that could pool the resources of its partners and facilitate the advancement of the Kingdom of God beyond the ability of a single person.

Today, FMIN has grown to over one-hundred-ninety partners, representing hundreds of churches, ministries, and businesses in thirty-three countries.

Vision

We are expanding the Kingdom of God by establishing local churches and translocal ministries, raising up spiritual leaders, networking with business ministers, and empowering all believers to walk in the fullness of their callings and giftings. We connect people and inspire dreams and vision through conferences, camps, mission trips, and resources such as newsletters, books, audio messages, and our website.

Newsletter

FMIN publishes a newsletter twice a year as a service to FMIN partners and their local ministries. We invite you to request a complimentary copy of our current edition by contacting us and supplying your complete mailing address. We would love for you to get to know us better and see what God is doing in our midst!

For more information about FMIN, events, and partnership; please contact us at:

FMIN
P.O. Box 609
Littleton, CO 80160
USA

Phone: (303) 777-1113
E-mail: info@fmin.org
Website: www.fmin.org

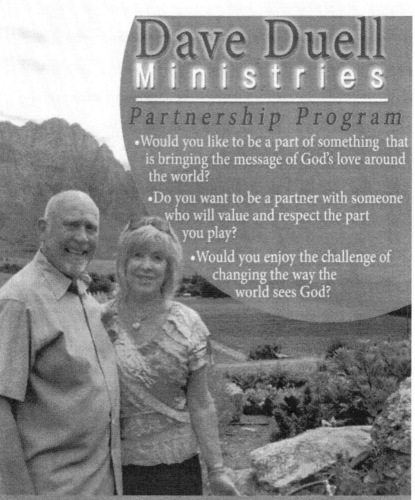

Dave Duell
Ministries
Partnership Program

- Would you like to be a part of something that is bringing the message of God's love around the world?
- Do you want to be a partner with someone who will value and respect the part you play?
- Would you enjoy the challenge of changing the way the world sees God?

If you answered yes to any of these questions, we would love to have you partner with us.

Together we are letting the world know that God loves them and there's nothing they can do to change that!

What do you receive as a monthly partner?

1. A monthly newsletter that keeps you up-to-date with relevant teaching and ministry projects
2. A free CD set
3. Faith Ministries International Network Newsletter published twice annually
4. Special Monthly Offers
5. Eternal deposits into your heavenly bank account

When you partner with Dave and Bonnie, you help make a difference in lives around the world.

Yes, Dave and Bonnie, I am partnering with you in letting the world know God loves them. My monthly gift will be:

$100 $75 $50 $25   other

My one-time gift: _____ I want to give by credit card.

My credit card # is: _____ Expiration date: _____

Name: _____

Address: _____

City: _____ State: _____ Zip: _____

Email: _____

I am already on your mailing list

Send me a free product catalog

Dave Duell Ministries
P.O. Box 609
Littleton, CO 80620
(303)777-1113   Fax: (303)777-9342
www.daveduell.com

Made in the USA
Charleston, SC
30 January 2013